❀❀❀❀❀❀❀❀❀❀❀❀❀❀❀❀❀❀❀❀❀❀❀❀

LUMINIST

Poetry by

V.T. Abercrombie

Cover by Wade Blissard

❀❀❀❀❀❀❀❀❀❀❀❀❀❀❀❀❀❀❀❀❀❀❀❀

BLACK BUZZARD PRESS
3503 Ferguson Lane
Austin, Texas 78754

ISBN 978-0-938872-40-5

For: John Abercrombie &

John Jr., Virginia Lee, Gil & Lorraine

Acknowledgements

I wish to thank the following for previous publication:
Borderlands - *Counting Beans,* and *The Old Black Iron Skillet,* California
Quarterly - *Monday,* the Cathartic - *Mother's Desk,* Cedar Rock - *Phantoms,*
Christmas in Texas - *Mere,* Concho River Review - *Messages From the Dead,*
Crab Creek Review - *Duck Hunt,* Dog River Review - *For Teresa,* Houston
Poetry Festival Anthology - *Homeless,* and *Kitchen Time,* Iodine - *Full Moon,*
Little Pear Press - *The Shell Game* and *The Great Blue Heron,* Main Street Rag -
Afternoon by the Pond, Days, the Size of Things, Floating Air, Indian Summer
and *Luminist,* Midway Review - *Anatomy of Sixteen,* Mississippi Arts & Letters -
Legacy, Poem - *Vail,* Poetry Fool - *Volplane* and *R-S-L Official...,* Pudding
House - *Boiling Jelly in...,* *Magic Act* and *The Drunk,* Roanoke Review –
Tanana, Rising Star - *Shadows/Beach,* Roswell Literary Review - *Color Blind,*
Slant - *Desert Rites,* Suddenly III - *Ross,* a Texas Christmas - *Noel Christmas
in Texas,* Texas Poetry Calendar - *Fall Foliage,* Visions-International -
Doppelganger, *Kitchen Time, Loss of UT Scholar...,* *Lucille Joy is Lost,*
Missing, One of Those Late Night Phone Calls.., Signing On and *The Sketch
Pad,* White Pelican - *Contemplations,* the Wounded Heart - *After the Fact,*

FIRST EDITION, April, 2009

TABLE OF CONTENTS

1. LIGHTS AND SHADOWS

2. LOSSES

6. "HERE AND GONE"

MÈRE

She was mère,
mother of my mother
silk dress, warm arms.
She orchestrated Christmas Eve.
"Move the blue light up higher.
Place the red light there, in the middle.
Bèbè, here's the crèche.
Be careful of *l'enfant*.
Get the egg-nog ready.
Its time to whip the cream.
Santa Claus will leave switches and ashes
for little girls who don't go to bed on time."
Mère held me in the green pine's
green smell, and I slept.

They call them plantation pines now.
Children in their twenties
come to decorate this tree.
Full branches hold old ornaments
in Christmas card serenity.
"Put the lights in close to the trunk.
Watch out for old Santa.
Hang him in the middle, high up."
Christmas tree lights shine
on my translucent children,
reed hollow.
Christmas carols distill the night—
yearly promises hold me
greenly, like the scent of pine.

NOEL

Blue spruce, the tree is in the stand,
filling the room with the smell
of Christmas. Smells that track

the past—when tinsel lay crinkled
and heavy on the hand, when bowls
of eggnog shone bright with beads

of sweat, Grandmère directed
decor, quieted arguments that
occasionally broke like ornaments

on the floor, when dolls occupied
spaces under the tree and grownups
smiled secret smiles at me. Tomorrow

we gather, roast turkey scenting the air,
Bloody Marys on silver trays chilling
crystal glasses, stuffed toys

and tricycles bulging under the tree,
chocolate in mugs, loud greetings, hugs,
maybe sharp words, all waiting. And,

waiting, we'll watch the children,
our grandchildren, hold ghosts in
their grasp, begin their long past.

LUMINIST

It takes shape like a painting—
It's just a spot, left lobe, don't worry, we'll watch it.
Gesso spreads over my raw canvas.
My daughters bring me color—Janis mixes blues,

the cool shades that organize her sons' games,
grades, take over most of my bookkeeping.
Barbara lives the reds, scarlets, her life vibrant
with a seven year old who climbs on roofs, stops up toilets.

From my bed the window yields
the green of spring, a view
of the house behind ours, torn down so quickly
that I can't remember how it looked,
I watch the birds,

mourning doves drinking from puddles,
mocking birds chasing the neighbor's cat.
I think I can see buds forming on the plants
in my zinnia bed.
Days don't sort themselves
out the way they used to. I have to ask,
What day is today?
Friends frame my time
with blue blooming iris, sun flowers,
the chocolate candy I used to love, offer funny stories
of the outside world. I still want to know,
What's the weather like today? Who's mad
at who? Why did he leave her? Was there someone else?

This morning the crows' shadows cross my
window, down the drive, swift like a dream.
Their wings, like airbrushes, dry the paint,
Today I leave for the hospital, my canvas
stretched tight, and I'll be done with death.

THE VIEW

She should be tall, six or seven feet,
some sort of durable stone or concrete—
my angel with half-spread wings—set
at the head of my grave, on guard,
imposing. The feathers delineated,
ready for flight. Her staid expression

will remind me of the time I got
my first quarter horse, of Grandmère's
comfort on the sleeping porch
her amused, *Let me go to sleep first,
child. Then I don't feel you kicking,*
the morning sound of the milk man's horse,
riding on the hard bar of Bob McClellan's
bicycle, Jerry Robison's hands on my
back when he kissed me, walking
down the aisle in St. John's chapel,
holding the first baby, my first good poem.

I will sit high in the big oak tree close by,
(the gnarled branches won't even poke
holes in my thighs) watch the life-mists
leak from some of the graves, like the volcano
site I saw in Hawaii, the ground giving
up smoke pillars to remind us of what's
underneath. I won't even mind when
they come in the gray-ash night to steal
my angel, three of them, sullen, young,
bent from the weight of the wings. Let her
help who she can. I'm gone.

POST CARDS IN AN OLD SHOE BOX

The old-style precise handwriting holds voices
from France, addressed to *Mon cher Henri,*
Adele Lavie, Ma chere petite Yvonne,
Gabrielle. Picture postcards from another
world sent from the past, signed with illegible
initials, names. Minute scribbled writing
covers both sides like fine needle point.

Photographs, sepia or gray, lure me—
Le Champs-Elysees, wide, horse drawn carriages
in promenade, *Le Havre-le bains Marie-Christine*
features people dressed in long dresses that sweep
the sand. Could Monet have painted that very
picnic? *Le pont du Commerce-La Bourse,*
no cars only pedestrians on that bridge.

Some dated, 1904, 1914. Lourdes1907,
full color Luxembourg1918 stamped
"passed as censored" says little, 1934...
I can't attend their hours, years.
I can't translate their emotions,
only a few of the words. Nor, who cares
for Henri, Gabrielle, Yvonne or how.

Nothing of war, no tears of loss mar
the stamps, dates and fine writing.
Each card stacked tight in the box
leaves its mark, treasures its moment,
exactly the way our unthinking
heartbeats measure breath.

AFTER THE FACT

Today
there seems to be plenty
of room—room to run, mourn,
have hysterics or what have you.
I move between immobile things,
houses, fences, bent skylines
on multi-story glass buildings,
and friends caught in attitudes
like the game Statue. I wave
my blue shirt like a windmill
shoving at air, stumbling
under skies set with stone clouds.
You are there, best-loved, mouth
open in a lie, caught in this
moment like a still life, "Family,
Friends and Roses."
Tonight
your untempered life scrapes
me with worries that scurry
in currents of air. And I no
longer move. Like sculpted rock,
feet apart, dressed in slacks
and sweater, I stand, smiling
a scream, remembering days
when all seemed in balance.
When I moved in tempo
and reflections were only glass.
Now memories march single file
the way ants tread a well-worn
trail. Line the hardened
runnels of my face giving the
appearance of tears.

VOLPLANE

I am sheeted cardboard
braced upright between two boulder sons.
They won't let me down to lie in rest.
They scribble directives
on my grey cardboard skin.
"Eat your dinner. Drink your juice.
Don't forget your pills."
It is written where their father
stepped on the dog, killing it.
Below that is noted his death.
Punched in blue ink leaving a hole,
he left me with two seven year sons.
The years have rolled me paper-thin.
I am swaddled in nylon
like exotic colored binding cloth,
wrapped in fancy fuzzy bathrobes
and made to rise again.
Enough yet.
I will never pick mayhaws again.
Let me down. Fold me in the middle,
twice over on each side.
Fling me. Let me fly.

R-S-L- OFFICIAL Badminton Shuttlecocks

*"This tar-lined container is humidified with HUPYDROLE... After
considerable research by R.S.L. Shuttlecocks Co— this humidifier
was found to be the most efficient means of preserving the natural
life of feathers..."*

Long, tubular shaped, a funny light olive
green color, imprinted with a gold coat
of arms, it was hidden behind thirty years
of fading, falling-apart photo albums.
Mother must have saved it. She was never
one for waste. How did it get to my house?

A message from beyond? Inside, clear
new-mint-white, with glue caramelized
on the quills, rounded ends wrapped
in green strips, the shuttlecocks come
out onto my tan Formica kitchen top,
their feathers aligned, unbattered.

For tournament play it says on the tube.
They played in the evenings, the grown ups,
in the lighted back yards, and we
children watched. Called birds, they
flew over the net in great arcs, almost
as soundless as my mother's night

crying. Hit with vicious power, they
sailed like slices of light from one
team to another. In my hand now,
weighing less than a thought. I'll
put those summer evenings in the glass
cabinet where I can see what I see.

INDIAN SUMMER (For My Mother)

I opened the closet today
where I store special things—
clothes that don't fit anymore,
too good to let go, a child's
tea set, assortments of family

watches. Your dress burgeoned
out, that great huge skirt made
for dancing, a riotous spring
of chiffon and orange tulle,
wrapping me in Dance City

memories where you made me
play mother, suffer recitals
in fox-trot time. Where strobe
lights dropped petals of platinum
across silver hair, swirled skirts

into flowers; where dance instructors,
like black-tuxed stems, gathered
partners in swirling bouquets,
I stood there awhile with a heart
like a trowel, digging at your smile.

THE SKETCH PAD

She said she wants to paint moving things,
wants to come to the pond in front of my
house, sketch the ducks. Come watch Sunday
dinner, I think. Observe Grandmère's ghost
riffling through her bone-handled knives as I
set the table. Watch me stir sauce with a bent

once-silvered spoon. Catch mother's shade, her
pursed lips, the shake of her head at the old spoon's
rust. And my grown children—seem to stand still,
quietly hold drinks, chat amiably. Get your pencil.
Work quickly. Their ghosts move between them, divide
the air, shed worries on my floor. Angry words

like hordes of gnats hum silently around their heads.
Did you see that? John's phantom arm punched his
brother-in-law. And me, do you see my specter? I'm
the one with the dust pan, chasing around them, bending
to brush up words, old grudges, the grit of unfounded
envies, dumping them in the garbage of my mind.

PHANTOMS

Others hear clankings
Peculiar ringing of bells
But my ghost
My ghost smells
Of faint talcum
Fresh from the tub
The tub with arrogant legs
Rough iron shell
Turning smooth porcelain lip
Inward
To hold a pumice stone
The stone rubbing smooth
Soothing
Soothing vapors edge me
lending me the touch
Of sun-stiff towels
For this cold day

SHADOWS/BEACH

Sand is my substance.
Morning-sun-black colors each grain.
Thinned edges define parameters
and contain this shade;

slice through the beach
cover ruts, slide me forward.
Flat, I am an acrobat, capable
of grace without effort.

My fingers are long.
My arms command magic.
My familiars, shadow seagulls,
swoop sand like unrestrained

shuttles gone mad without a weaving.
Sharp in silhouette, they pierce
foam and sand, dangling cries of sky,
make of me their loom.

FULL MOON

Shiny disc, perfectly round, like certain
childhood days - sitting on iced concrete
steps, the feel of my cousin's winter coat,

now mine, jumping cracks on roller skates.
Mother's warmth when I hurt. No steps
marred your surface. Your mystery prevailed,

cheese and jumping cows, moon, full moon,
your pale glow rinses off bad days, soaks
me in your light, an immersion of heart.

ANATOMY OF SIXTEEN

So thin
Elongated bones matched against time
Stretch skin like a surgeons glove
The knob of a heart pulses a protest
Indentations end sharply
Forbid my arms
Knees are wide angled
bent against reason
Ribs move notes in ivory cipher
Attached at the breast
Like a pulley bone
To be broken
Make a wish

THE SINS OF THE...

The woman walking in front of me wears
my roommate's hips, high, up around her waist,
straight down to her legs. Her head, rounded, bears
short hair, sits her neck the way my roommate's
did. She turns a face, unknown, a stranger.
Whose fleshed-out skin covers her borrowed bones?
What family tree yields her doppelganger?
Are there many of us, clay figures thrown,
mass produced, on some thoughtless potters wheel?
And you, heartbreak of my life, drunk son, man,
call again, demand hope I cannot feel.
Artists call it negative space, the span
between objects. Not empty, an outline
filled with the rage of sameness, not yours, mine.

DOPPELGANGER

I put your name, *China Zorilla*, in the search
bar and there you were, Uruguay, actress
of renown, starring in a new play about love

at eighty. Rosa, our tour guide in Montevideo,
ran to me, called your name, *China, China Zorilla.*
You are her twin, she said. I had never heard

of you then. I see your photographs now,
China. Plays, movies, television. Your skin
covers my mother's face, the nose could be

Grandmere's, your natural hair looks to be mine.
Is your heart round and smooth or cracked
and creviced like mine? Are we connected

in time by French ancestors, some thread of
a great design? Or did a creator, bored by
it all, simply get tired of making new faces?

CONTEMPLATIONS OF AN ADOPTED CHILD

My ghosts arrange clouds on sunny
days, soft totems shaped like the uncle
who lost his dukedom—his nose
protrudes straight from his forehead
in the manner of a Roman coin, an
aunt who almost won the Nobel Prize
for science, Mother, rounded with love—
her mouth hollow with songs unsung,
Father, young, athletic, lost without
a son to play catch, teach to hunt,
play the guitar, drive a car.

My ghosts follow me to work,
as I pick up my son, take him
to basketball practice, teacher
conferences, detention. Watch
us do homework, stare like startled
hares when I punish him, gawk
as I lose my temper, go crazy
with discipline. My daughter wastes
no time with phantoms, would never
hear music from the past. Lacrosse

is her game and I'm not in it. Her
nose differs from mine, her hair,
thick, curly, unlike her mother's,
must be a gift from my mother or
some great, great. I look through
the bones of my children, the shape
of their heads until my sight blurs
the way cumulous clouds flatten,
cover the sky, and wait, wait for
grandchildren to show me
the faces of all my old ghosts.

MAGIC ACT

I call you up and you are there—
well dressed in your sport coat,
slacks and shirt: cleanly edged, reflecting
neat like my empty crystal goblets.
I am not a user of witchcraft employing
sacrificial stones, daggers and drums.
I am the conjurer of the kitchen with peanut butter sandwiches,
milk and cookies. My hand on your head drew you up from
childhood, eased your pains with its balms of Great Shakes.
I am the mage at the sink casting down demons,
pulling out hamburgers, catsup
and hand written excuse notes.

The telephone signals your late night call and madness begins.
Doves fly from the pans, smoke leaves messages in dirt in the
refrigerator exhaust, the disposal grinds air, bright knotted
dish towels fall to the floor, grease
sputters pentagrams on the back of my hands.
The sawtooth knife used to cut the lady in two
cuts ragged and leaves fibers of guilt, strong like the invisible
wires that levitate love and hold it in defiance of fact.

DAYS

Like a still life, the shelf under the kitchen windows
holds a two-drawer plastic bin filled with bills,
an aloe vera plant, useful for burns, the phone,
of course, catalogs stacked with wishful thoughts,
literary magazines tagged on the page where my
poem appears, a bowl of bananas topped with

two tomatoes, the square, painted cloth "Happy
Mother's Day" given me the year the youngest
didn't drink, framed family pictures. I remember
the day that walked him back to the street, the picture
of us all, missing only one; the day's set of shoulder
when older son brought Lorraine's smile

home, the day that posed us in front of mountains;
the way days chug by, grandchildren grow, shift
like dust on the shelf. A bookmark of memories,
written small the way my French aunts used to
cover post cards until there was no space left,
to put in the not-finished novel on the counter.

SNOW BLINDNESS

They call you grown,
Child. Your shape
In my arms, sweet-skin
Cheek—myopic memories,
Like cataracts, blur
My vision, hamper focus.

Negative space outlines
Your edges, forms a
Figure I cannot see.
August burns with
Birthdays and you are
Grown child. Blind,

Drugged white, your
Cut-out contour can't
Be held. Time has
Inhaled words for a high
Puffed on my pain and
Dreamed our past to smoke.

THE DRUNK

I smell your sweet childhood flesh
in the green of pine needles around
the pond. They fall like memories—
rocking you, dressing you, feeding you
morsels of dinner—then turn tan, crust

the grass, a nuisance to be raked,
disposed of in green plastic leaf bags.
Your phone calls trail fumes of helpless
need, not deciduous like the pines but
sharp, sticky, they pierce time, affection.

MISSING

Daughter, daughter—daughter that can't be,
daughter that never was—a face, profiled
pure as the queen of England's, struck

on the coin of my life—I call you from memory,
what I was to my mother and she to hers
and hers and hers and hers. The words fall—

clouds like puddled milk—filling the valley
between us. And still the green tops
of loneliness jut past as if between us

the runes remain unread, untranslated;
the look, passed between eyes reading
a joke, seeking agreement, that singular

moment when one is allowed to glimpse
a thought, slides formlessly like molten metal
before it's cast. My arms recall rocking

you, my fingers trace ridges of touch when
touch was enough—mockeries of my constructed
smile when we talk our counterfeit talk.

FOR TERESA

Your car was like a concert—
live, loud, sound-filled
vibrations racing at love;
cut off, ended on highway 71
by an eighteen wheeler truck.
Your flesh bonded with sheet metal—
an eighteen wheeler for a marriage bed.

A union proposed by some inept god
who thought to recreate you
by smashing you back to skin,
bones, gristle and blood.
Except for your hand, your
folded hand. Asking what?

Another chance, for your guitar
placed just so, your blue hair brush
to shine your hair, a ring
for your finger, our forgiveness?
Daughter, daughter, your hand, your
supplicant hand reaches all my fears
and lays like steel against my bones.

MONDAY

I am the oracle of kitchen.
My disposal rumbles and gods speak
over grape stems, banana peels
and chrysanthemums with crayon-yellow petals.
I hear the voice in my interpretations of choice.
I feed it last night's arguments,
sharded words and lost lust;
chop up tears with broken egg shells.
Gods whine with the confluence of yesterday's effluence
in a mighty joining of minced souls,
sewer sludge trolls and profiteroles.
Assembled again by crazy king's men,
Tuesday's reconstituted souls sing me Wednesday's prophecy.
Take my offering.
Let no one listen.
I hear the song.

COUNTING BEANS

The beans have burned again,
scorched tight to the bottom
of the pan. Stuck the way

Mickey won't pull her table
far enough out from the wall
so we have to scrunch around

to move for bridge; like the thirty
tardy minutes Lee takes from
everyone, Aunt Dot's firm refusal

to listen, John's bitter bickering
with his ex-wife. I need the Brillo
pad, steel wool with soap, to

clean and scrape and scrub my
charcoaled habits, find the black
enameled bottom once again.

THE OLD BLACK IRON SKILLET

Skittered, skittered is the word for
the thought that's lost, the profound
one that would make the perfect poem,

the way the lives, Grandmère, Grandpere,
Aunt Dot, Uncle Herve, Mother, Father,
the baby aunt, dead at birth, flicker

and flare in my mind, connect my
black iron skillet that holds the smoke
of family dinners, okra and tomatoes,

cornbread and, of course, fried chicken
to family fights, Uncle Herve's unhappiness,
his move back to the family home,

Aunt Dot's childlessness. Tonight I'll heft
that skillet, cook onions in grease, splatter
skittish words for tomorrow's poem.

KITCHEN NIGHTS

Thoughts, like wet coffee grounds
clump on the sides of sleep
rearranging the swell of my dreams.
My mother, strong French features, is
stirring the pot on the stove while
she waits for my father to come home.
He's late, she says, but he'll be here
soon. Business, you know. And the smell
of dinner dims our nerves until the sound
of his car rackets in the driveway,
and the clove tucked sideways in his
mouth battles puffs of bourbon when he
talks and filters his smile through
the past. My skin stretches over
the bones of my father the way dinosaurs
are put together fragment by fragment
while the voices are Grandmère
and Grandpère, remembered like the light
that erased childhood nightmares.
There's plenty of room to skid around
corners of ancestors. Why wasn't
the other grandfather ever mentioned,
absent the way a hearing loss diminishes
sound? They said my father visited
his mother every day at lunch, a faithful son.
And the atmosphere thickens and my
bones rebel, realign themselves,
straighten like mother's long handled
spoon, the better to stir the morning.

KITCHEN TIME

Bread, the staff to hold a life together, rustic
wheat, sourdough, French, sits on my dining
table as do Grandmère's pearl handled knives,

dull, worn out, shaky in their settings. The smell
of barbecue sauce on chicken, charcoal smoke,
crudities of green peppers, tomatoes mingle

with my families' smiles and hidden thoughts—
*Can my marriage last? Can ex wife ruin your
life? Is my child headed for trouble? Does*

*bankruptcy last forever? Will I ever find another
man?* I cut up onions with Mother's rusty steel
knife, stir the soup with her bent ladle, pour it

into Tante Lily's chipped bowls, shake up
new generations like Grandmère's vinegar
and oil dressing, hold close this family's savor.

BOILING JELLY IN SARATOGA, TEXAS

We called you spry, strong. You could
hoist grandchildren long after you should.
I see you, old mother, the way you lean
down, pick that twig up off the ground,

keep your vegetable patch clean of debris.
Clean as your mind when you search my
name. *Who are you? What do I call you?*
Old mother, gathering wits like the mayhaws

you collected to fill this mason jar—jelly,
rose-red and translucent. Shroud-like sheets
hold your bones, tubes and needles knit
a kind of crèche, drape your empty shape.

Mercifully, Brother Beard forgot his glasses
And cut his sermon short. He never would
have known to speak about the wayward
light that pours through my empty jelly jars.

MOTHER'S DESK

Checkbook records, pictures, childhood diaries,
postcards, letters, retain a paper soul.
The bottom right drawer
is filled with ancestors.
Ancestors entombed in small file folders.
Grandmère, paper whispers recall
the force of her arms and her religion.
Grandpère's life rustles out;
born Le Havre, France, a cotton broker,
dying he stayed alive to nurse his wife.
A single newspaper article crackles open.
The other grandmother; pictured sere and worn,
a girl when Wilson's raiders stole
her family's livestock, came to Texas,
had ten children, one of them my father.
My father,
faded grudges are folded in his file
best left to yellow into forgiveness.
Thank you letters done, I lay my mother's
packet in. Close the drawer.
Gracious curved, old-timey, the lady's desk
was owned by my grandmother.. my mother...
is mine.

GRANDMÈRE'S DESK

The drawer in Grandmère's desk is deep. Piled folders stack up lives
that ordinarily wouldn't touch. Each French grandparent, Grandpère,
Grandmère, fills a brown mottled, cracking folder—telegrams, notes,
cards, lists of those present for the funeral. Grandpère's lists him

as a cotton man, president of Allgeyer Cotton Company, lists
remaining relatives, shows his father's name. The mother's line is blank.
My father's folder lodges in the middle like a disturbance
of light. Last to die, Mother presides at the top—her folder, white,

still-soft imitation leather. Yellowed and torn, a long obituary is what
is known of my father's mother—described as *living a noble
and well-spent life* (ten children) *symbolic of the unselfish
and uncomplaining spirit of the women of the Reconstruction.* Her

picture seems sere. She's slight with pulled back hair, black dress. And where
is my father's father? When did he die? of what? It mentions what he did.
Singer Sewing Machine Company, not when or how long. I never
knew them. Barely knew the brothers and sisters. (My father never got along.)

Scraps of paper in a drawer—dim like old survey maps that show a bent tree
now lost to lightning a pile of rocks now scattered, a fallen log canted
just-so over a stream that's meandered way off—make some sort of sense
to a map maker, keep one from endless circling in a mist of powdered bones.

LEGACY

It sits on my desk, the family album,
black cover, gray pages filled
with pictures held in place with black
triangles, my childhood, left to me

when mother died. Sepia photos
of great aunts, uncles, grand parents,
myself on tricycle, in Easter dress,
at Christmas, Mother, Father.

Father dressed for hunting, smiling
with dead deer, holding racks of birds.
My thoughts, fast as doves at waterhole
shooting time, come slanting in, cutting

soundless air—Of the space between
the snapshots, of mother, sitting home
alone, Christmas Eve at the window
watching for his car, calling Aunt

Ruth to find him. All the faces
faded now, and memories, like
the sound of a shotgun too long shot,
cause a certain deafness of the heart.

THIRTY DAYS HAS NOVEMBER...

It sits on my desk, the calendar,
this month in view. Each day preens
in its square, some clear, others—

my illegible handwriting clouds
their countenance like a design
by a preschooler—*poetry-me, bridge
lesson, dinner/Weatheralls, Dr. Greer.*

It sits on last year's datebook. I can
check—*When did I go to the dentist,
the skin doctor, Sara's birthday?*

Months darken as I turn their pages.
Turned face down, they thin to October,
leave edges curled to December.

The days file my notes, squiggled
writing, preludes, possibilities,
prospects. Next year's calendar waits,
its history slick with unsupported years.

SIGNING ON

You write your name the same
each time now. We can open
you a checking account my father
said. My signatures, sprawled
across the bottom of each check—
clothes, midnight pizzas to doctor
bills, groceries, mortgage payments—

all spawn the same checkbook look.
In mother's desk I found a book,
small, dated 1911-1917, called "My
Friends," filled with signatures
written perpendicular on the page, each
folded while the ink was wet. Like a Rorsach
test, dragons, butterflies, angels engaged

the inky names. I imagine each looped L,
each turn of a P, duplicating itself through
World War I, The Great Depression,
the way soldiers are taught to march
holding arms at a just-so angle. Given
substance one could stack a life's
worth of signatures one over the other,

could see all the way down through
the Os and Ds to the beginning of it all.
Whether cursive or print, we lock ourselves
to life by the slant of an A, the swirl
of a B, the curve of an S, by the butterflies
and dragons and angels on yellowed paper
and the trail of signature bones behind us.

COLOR BLIND

You speak
Dove, colored, taupe,
smoky, silver and lead-gray.
Come, let me cover,
with glazes of color,
your chiaroscuro world.
Walk with me cobalt blue
toward limb-lined trees
graphed against bright light.
Smell sap-green furled leaves
        opening.
Watch your feet pantomime
in reds to Spanish rhythms.
Feel the yellows
        in washes of tears,
interrupted brine
against your face.
Remember
tasting honey pink
on your morning pancakes.
We'll find orange
        on beaches
in waves pulling sand
away from our toes.
Fights are purple
staining words
amethyst and royal.
But best is brown
When we are brown
in one warm skin
puddles of color.

DESERT RITES
(Arizona Dawn)

Old Hopi spirit,
your mountains,
scissor-cut, against
a blue glass sky,
backdrop the distant
traffic's dust blossoms
that flower and spread
past the peripheries
of your land. Golf
courses green your

desert the way feathers
brighten a rain dance.
If I hold out my arms,
half of a circle,
I'm a dowsing rod,
turning like a drill
in the dunes. Sand-soft,
my feet pattern the rills,
stir centennials
of spirits, ancient

tribal lore, medicine men.
Will you answer with deep
clouds loomed from
the past, shuttle them
through my air-linked
arms, cause sudden rain
to erase the dawn and
scythe the dust, weave
me a memory of morning
fragile as a sand drawing?

AFTERNOON BY THE POND
(Scientists dissect bird wings, learn to make machines fly.)

The old wooden glider stirs summer air, grass,
magnolia blossoms, jasmine, moves it toward
the heron's nest, a frowzy baby perched on
top—not a flyer yet. One parent, wings as wide
as a fighting kite, drops to the shore. I suspect
take-out minnows for fledglings. Summertide
rides wings of smaller birds, doves, swallows,
cardinals, weaves invisible messages between
trees, across the pond. Crows interrupt with caws
of *me, me, me.* And I watch, rock, share
altered air, think me too, me too, me too,
and know, somehow, it's all a matter of wings.

DUCK HUNT

Last night's dreams remain
rumpled in my just-left bed.
Dark morning frost covers
the prairie, and seeps
like a leaky nightmare into my lungs.
Cold moves in waves against my waders
as I set painted decoys on the water.
The retriever runs a trail on shore
just as he does in his afternoon naps.
Our blind, a sunken metal drum,
holds the chill of sleep.
Ducks pattern the sky
like buckshot from an open choke.
Decoys bob a welcome while
I chuckle a feeding call.
They pass, high, turn,
drawn to water and feeding flocks.
My shots cover the morning.
Two fall. The rest slice high
into clouds and are gone.
"Fetch." His jump spans ancestors...
The black dog lands swimming into
side-floating mallards, day bright now—
day-bright for running down dreams
in the Labrador's feathered mouth.

VAIL

Consider the mountain, heaved out like bile
from some fiery mouth a millennium
ago, worn down, and raised once more, housing wild
animals, then Indians. Yet to come
was Lord Gore. Came with his entourage, wagons
and servants, to conquer this range of the
Rockies, bringing the civilization
of England to the West. Consider me,
skier, attacking the mountain, riding
the chair lift, gondola and snowmobile,
outfitted with skis, arms out, legs sliding
down meadows, past stands of firs, in bright teal
parka and pants racing time infester
of the mountain. Consider, consider...

FLOATING AIR

The view from the moon
is green, and steps are
weighted to prevent
flight, uncertain drifts
to the right or left.

consigned to gravity,
nightmares chased our
childhood until our feet
felt flight and with great
effort we flew our dreams.

We still dream of flying,
spread our arms in hang
gliders, slide down
the mist, jump
with parachutes the way

a spider unravels his line,
dare the air, slicing it
into pie-shaped pieces
with our outstretched
limbs. Some of us jump

from buildings—trusting
the slow wingbeats
of pelicans, the lazy
turns of a buzzard,
thinking we'll waft

like leaves in the fall.
While in the swift drift
of our body we plan
for a future, embossing
our spirit on earth.

THE GREAT BLUE HERON IS A ...

Two blue herons, sentinels, unmoving,
on a high pine branch, observe us, me
on the glider, grandson, grandfather
putting large plastic sacks filled with
minnows and perch into the pond. Do
they calculate the distance the fish will
swim, the effect of sudden change, how
long it will take the minnows to find
the shallow shore, to be dinner? Blurred
in the crook of two limbs like my memories
of you, the twiggy nest holds the herons
future. The splash of released water, ripples
of fish glinting like bits of broken glass,
the herons deep raspy call, a flash of
wings, cloud shards of late-night regrets.

NIGHT MOVES

Back then we hunted coons, rode
the pasture from the back of a pickup,
shone the spotlight over trees, watched
for two reflections, eyes, white, bright,

beams. *No, wait, they're green. Spider*
eyes. Now, there, quick, shoot. We
got 'em. Sudden dark. At Jennie's
house they stand outside her sliding door,

black-masked like a joke, shiny eyes,
looking helpless and cute, begging
for scraps which she provides. Outside
my bedroom, the motion detector light

goes on and off all night. If I get up
quick, sometimes I can see the raccoon
amble off, his nocturnal business just begun.
Down by the edge of the pond, the ducks

huddle into sleep, feathers fluffed, heads
under wings. The coon helps himself to warm
eggs held in those little paws. The light
shutters off, leaves only the sudden dark.

COON HUNT

It takes shape like a thought
niggling at the edges of sleep slips
its light across my mind displaying
one o'clock—time for coon hunting
in the country, pick-ups and tequila,
close jouncing bodies, a union
of guns and back country roads

when nights, dark like blindness,
accept the spotlight splaying
across limbs and leaves, searching—
not for the green of spider eyes,
for warm blooded eyes, butter
colored, twin reflections, high
in trees, raccoon eyes, open, curious,

shot with the 22 rifle or the 357 magnum.
Like horses in nippy weather, we run,
gather beneath the tree, see the striped
mound, pillowed and loose,
toss it in the back of the pick-up...
Eyes closed, light-lined, curled
in my bed, I dig at the dark, at sleep.

FALL FOLLIAGE
(for Ruby Jo)

In October, hill country
leaves startle the senses
with color—amber, salmon,

rose to red and downright yellow.
Trees quilt the mountains
and crayola the roadsides.

Not a good time to die, Ruby Jo.

You would breathe the air,
crisp as a new deck of cards,
pull out your calendar, ask,

"When can we play, huh?"
Remember, we played
bridge in Galveston, admired

the lights next door, the way
they hovered above the water,
not your gaudy red, green

and blue ones, but soft, somehow
European in feeling, golds, mauves
and an occasional red. Made

us think of villas and dukes
and exotic evenings. Ruby,
Ruby Jo, where will we get

a fourth for odd jokes, for
bidding fights, someone who
understands the clarity of color?

MESSAGES FROM THE DEAD

Houdini devised a secret message
he would send after death.
Bess, his wife, waited but none
came. Too complicated I think,
all those codes between them.

I mean, how can a spirit think all
that through. Mother simply used lights,
lamps, chandeliers, blinking
them at will. She hung around
for about a month. It was
comforting to know she was still
in touch. Abel and Ruth finally
told her, Yvonne, that's enough.
You're scaring us. Never one
to cause trouble, lights ceased
stuttering, went back to uneasy
incandescence.

Sara's dead husband knocked his
toothbrush off the bathroom
shelf in his communiqué.
I grieved for Elaine until
the night my sleeping skin
tightened with an odd prickle.
I knew she was saying,
Get over it. I'm gone but it's O.K.

There must be some sort of waiting
period, so many deaths; how can they
all be processed at once, much like
the wait for a new driver's license?
I don't think I'll be allowed the messages
my family doesn't want to hear,
Quit being so pessimistic.
Try to think about your money
before you spend it. You're
hanging in, don't take that drink.
They plug their ears to all my codes
today. I guess the best I can do
when I go is, maybe,
melt the ice in their drinks for a while.

ONE OF THOSE LATE NIGHT PHONE CALLS
THAT SCARE YOU TO DEATH

She called—his wife, Bernie's wife—to find out when he was
an Eagle Scout. What year. Did I remember Bernie? Grade
school. Recess. He was there. Quiet. Just there.
Tenderfeet, they called them. The ones at the beginning,
scouts without pins, projects half done. How would I know
when Bernie made Eagle Scout? A biography,
Bernie's biography.

He died two years ago. She's writing it. Cataloging his
life. For his children she said. There must be a second
or third grade class picture with Bernie in it--or do they
fade away, those round faces sprouting souls like potato
eyes in the dimples of their fat. Her voice, smooth the
way a VCR rewinds let me imagine her never-told thoughts.

He made love to me first in the back seat
of his dad's car I hated it. Messy.
My back was sore for a week.

No, not that. She'll paste the pictures of their
wedding in the front. Her gown, long with a train,
preserved with heirloom wrap, on the top shelf
of her closet to be used by her daughter if she
ever marries. Baby pictures of the kids, Bernie,
still round faced, hairy in mustached manhood,
probably around 1961, holding the youngest,
a boy finally. She's the one behind the camera,
snapping life before it gets away.

The kids fight. Bernie works late. Henrv kissed
me behind the barbecue pit. squeezed my breast.
put his hand between my legs.

Bernie's picture at the annual company picnic.
Twenty five of them. Choose one.

The last time we made love—I can't remember
Between the television. beer and the
baseball games there wasn't much time.

She'll put in a poem about devotion edged with a design. And
find someone to tell her--which year he made Eagle Scout.

LOSS OF UH SCHOLAR IN CRASH ...
(University of Houston English professor,
Robert Wren. who died in a plane crash in Hawaii...)

Oh no, here comes Bobby Wren,
tall, ungainly, my only partner
in Mrs. Fanthom's fifth grade dance
class----Professor Robert Wren

who died taking time with him.
Years have passed like tissue paper
sheets crumpled loudly, carelessly,
stored the way old sweaters are,

stuffed deep in a drawer, left
to molder holey and forgotten, until
someone dies, takes away a piece of past.
It makes you look, begin to search,

think about the count. How many are
there, torn and wadded, used and new,
mindlessly crushed together? How can
I see to extricate one from the other,

carefully pull out the good, smooth
the wrinkles with care, lap them like
old dance cards, lay them over gaps as
the light lessens and the music gets louder?

LUCILLE JOY IS LOST.

They moved her to another nursing home
and I don't know her son's last name.
Joy was hers when she married again,
left behind the stalwart wife she'd been,
wrote poetry. She never called when joy
wore out, after she left her house to live
in the Assisted Living Place. I heard she
was fine, had a man-patient friend. Then
she was gone. I wonder if Death has found
her. Devious Death has a closet full of
costumes, white doctor's coats, a trainman's
uniform when he holds up the crossbar;
he uses drunken drivers, counsels suicides,
urges paradise on bombers, sneaks in when
you're sleeping. Maybe she's hiding out,
found herself another beau. Lucille could
always charm a man, even Death.

THE SHELL GAME

Like a duffle bag, loosely packed,
just this side of worn out, you
appear on my doorstep. *Yes?*
I say. You give a little wave.
With a con man's smile and sleight
of hand you shift the walnut shells
again the way a tattered beard,
ancient eyes can hide the misplaced
child I finally recognize. Your
clothes. You say you want them.
In your arms my hopes, folded
between useless garments,
travel with you to the street,
discarded like yesterday's promise.

ORSO
(Bear)

You've used our yard again,
a path from your den to food
down the mountain. I would
never suspect your presence
except for the scat you left
by the corner of the house.

Your passage is quiet. The air
never moves, seems to close
around your form, fill in quiet
space when you pass through
thick rhododendrons, pick
your way among sleeping day
lilies, dig at grub worms in the
hostas' bed along the driveway.

Elaine, what I notice most
about your lack of being is
the plump presence of memory,
memory that bumps me
suddenly—eye contact for
hidden laughter, morning phone
calls reviewing our husbands'
faults, children's problems,

the weight gain of two pounds
overnight, Thanksgiving plans.
Sister of the heart, your passage,
still now, quickens time, leaves me
only fugitive signs of your path.

ROSS

He never heard his mother's voice, his father's scolding
tones. He learned to plow in silent rows, gathered eggs
without the raucous fuss of squawking hens. When his
parents died he grunted grief and lived alone; brought
water from the noiseless creek; killed deer from a soundless
gun. Saturdays he drove his tractor to the road, hitched a
ride to town, bought groceries in the still of day, drank
whisky at the bar, watched mouths move and wondered
why. Grizzled men would bring him back, leave him by
his tractor. Emptied of his life, new owners found the cabin
walls held up like lumpy wallpaper by the tiny stapled bones
of raccoon penises. They wondered did he feel the sounds,
vibrations or was this message just a count of days and death?

HOMELESS

You stand in my office,
thinning hair, still blond,
beard skimpy as an adolescent's,
nice jacket-from Goodwill I suppose—
stained blue jeans, torn running shoes,
the stench of last night's drunk,
a cartoon character marked

20th Century Wastrel. No problem
getting here, a short hop
from the camp under the bridge.
You say, *They 're going to close
it down next month; where will
I go, what will I do?* I look down
at my shoes, newly laced, exactly

two crosses up, then under the slits
in the tongue to two more crosses,
tied, like my life—boy scouts,
high school, college, navy, work,
college, marriage, work; think
about the rehabs, worries, lawyers,
wasted love that spilled like beer

absorbed by the street. *I need help.
I'm hungry. They beat me up again
last night. I had to go to the hospital.*
This office, my office—phone lines,
connect times, Compuserve, AOL,
faxes, E-Mail, http://www.name.com.
Today the system's down.

HANGING A SIGN

Basil leaves in my herb pot sport
black spots. Not too good in salads.
But look at its shadow, sun-hard,

on the wooden fence—perfect leaves.
Somewhere you walk a street, hold
a sign I can't read. From a distance

you probably look pretty good,
your eyes clear, face stubble
hidden like the dirt on your shirt.

Signs around town say, *Help,
lost job, Homeless, Don't judge,
need job, Homeless Vet, God bless.*

One placard admits, *I need a drink.*
Wheel chairs, crutches crowd corners.
Men wave windshield scrubbers

As if to erase the night's hard edges—
plastic sacks, dozing humans under
the underpass. Go ahead, go ahead,

print your cardboard square with the
the ink of my sleepless nights. And I'll
say to you, not too good in salads.

TANANA

(The Tanana Indians built small houses about the size of dog houses over their graves. Each family had a special color and no names were ever inscribed. The Alaska Historical Society has restored this graveyard that we are about to see.

Guide for Alaska Tours)

Sleep cold, child.
Bear and wolverine
roam over us tracking
other prey, displace
snow with their prints,
sniff bright paint
on our totems, and
wander away winters.

Paths widen in summer,
bordered with outpourings
of green, room for strangers
to walk, talking other
languages, wearing odd
clothes, calling our name,
Tanana, Tanana.

Sleep another fall, child.
Bones of our fathers
weather with us, wars,
loves, dust and dirt.
Sleep—we sleep, motes
in a slippage of stars.